IT'S NOT YOUR SIGN
IT'S YOUR PATTERN

Why Attachment Styles Matter More
Than Compatibility in Love

Johanna Sparrow

Blue Shoes Publishing

IT'S NOT YOUR SIGN—IT'S YOUR
PATTERN Copyright © 2026 by Johanna
Sparrow
All rights reserved.

No part of this book may be reproduced,
distributed, or transmitted in any form or by any
means, including photocopying, recording, or
other electronic or mechanical methods, without
the prior written permission of the publisher,
except in the case of brief quotations embodied
in reviews.

Published by
Blue Shoes Publishing

This book is intended for informational and
inspirational purposes only. It is not a substitute
for professional mental health, medical, or legal
advice.

First Edition

Printed in the United States of America

TABLE OF CONTENTS

INTRODUCTION

You thought it was your sign.

You thought it was compatibility.
You thought it was timing.
You thought it was them.

But the truth is—

you've been repeating patterns you didn't
even realize you were in.

Love isn't supposed to feel confusing.

Yet somehow… it does.

The same feelings.
The same cycles.
The same endings.

Different person.
Same outcome.

At some point, you start to ask yourself:

"Why does this keep happening to me?"

And instead of looking inward—

you look outward.

You check signs.
You check compatibility charts.
You try to understand them.

But rarely do you stop and ask:

"What am I bringing into this?"

This book isn't here to blame you.

It's here to **wake you up**.

Because the truth is—

your zodiac sign may explain your
tendencies…

but your **attachment style explains your
patterns**.

And patterns?

They don't change just because the person
does.

If you don't become aware of them—

you will continue to relive them.

This is where everything shifts.

In these pages, you'll begin to see:

Not just who you've been choosing…

but **why you've been choosing them**.

Not just how you love…

but **how you've been sabotaging love
without realizing it**.

And once you see it clearly—

you won't be able to unsee it.

That's the moment your life changes.

Not because love becomes easier…

but because **you become more aware**.

More intentional.
More aligned.

And from that place—

you stop choosing what feels familiar…

and start choosing what feels right.

This isn't about your sign.

This is about your **pattern**.

And this time—

you're going to see it clearly.

CHAPTER ONE

Why You Keep Choosing the Same Person

You don't keep meeting the wrong people by accident.

It feels like chance.
It feels like bad luck.
It feels like timing.

But it's not.

There's a pattern.

Different face.
Different story.
Same feeling.

The same connection that feels strong in the beginning.
The same emotional pull you can't explain.
The same moments that make you believe,
"This one is different."

And then—

the same confusion.

The same distance.
The same heartbreak.

At some point, you start to question
everything.

"Why does this keep happening to me?"

And the answer isn't what you've been told.

It's not just about compatibility.
It's not just about your zodiac sign.
It's not even just about the other person.

It's about what feels familiar to you.

✨ Familiar Doesn't Mean Healthy

You are naturally drawn to what you
recognize.

Not what's best for you.
Not what's aligned for you.

What's familiar.

Familiar feels safe—even when it hurts.

If inconsistency is what you've experienced,
you'll feel a pull toward inconsistency.

If emotional distance is what you've known,
you'll feel drawn to people who keep you at
a distance.

If love has felt like something you had to
earn,
you'll be attracted to people who make you
work for it.

Not because that's what you want—

but because that's what your system
recognizes.

And what your system recognizes…

it trusts.

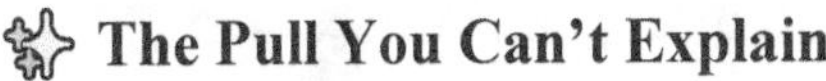 **The Pull You Can't Explain**

Have you ever met someone and felt an instant connection?

Something about them just feels right.

You can't explain it.
You don't even know them that well.

But something inside you says:

"This feels familiar."

That feeling isn't random.

It's your pattern activating.

It's your emotional blueprint recognizing something it already understands.

And that's why it's so hard to walk away.

Because you're not just connecting to the person—

you're connecting to a feeling you've known before.

✤ Chemistry Isn't Always a Good Sign

We've been taught to chase chemistry.

That instant spark.
That intense connection.
That feeling of *"I can't get enough of this person."*

But chemistry can be misleading.

Sometimes, what you call chemistry is actually:

- emotional familiarity
- unresolved patterns
- attachment activation

That intense pull?

It can come from a place that hasn't healed yet.

And when you don't understand that—

you confuse intensity with alignment.

🌠 You're Not Choosing Wrong—You're Choosing Unconsciously

This is where things begin to shift.

You're not just randomly picking the wrong people.

You're choosing based on:

- what feels familiar
- what feels emotionally activating
- what aligns with your internal pattern

And most of the time—

you're not even aware you're doing it.

You're not thinking:

"Let me choose someone who will repeat my past."

But your pattern is.

❧ The Cycle Looks Different—But It Feels the Same

It doesn't matter how different the person is on the surface.

They may:

✓ look different
✓ act different in the beginning
✓ say different things

But the emotional experience?

It repeats.

You end up feeling:

- unsure
- anxious
- disconnected
- misunderstood

And eventually—

you find yourself in the same place you've been before.

Wondering how you got there again.

✨ This Is Where Awareness Begins

The moment you recognize the pattern—

everything changes.

Not immediately.

But permanently.

Because once you see it…

you can't ignore it anymore.

You begin to question:

- why you feel pulled to certain people
- why some connections feel stronger than others
- why "good on paper" doesn't always feel right

And most importantly—

you begin to see your role in the cycle.

✨ It's Not About Blame—It's About Awareness

This isn't about blaming yourself.

It's about understanding yourself.

Because when you understand your patterns—

you gain power.

Power to pause.
Power to question.
Power to choose differently.

✨ The Truth You've Been Missing

You've been trying to figure out:

👉 who is right for you

When the real question is:

👉 **what pattern are you repeating?**

Because until you answer that—

you'll keep finding yourself in the same story…

just with a different person.

✨ A Moment of Reflection

Take a moment and ask yourself:

- What do my past relationships have in common?
- How do I usually feel in the beginning… and at the end?
- What type of person am I consistently drawn to?

Be honest with yourself.

Because the answers you avoid…

are the ones that reveal your pattern.

✾ What Comes Next

Now that you've seen the possibility of a pattern—

the next step is understanding **why it exists**.

Because your patterns didn't just appear.

They were formed.

Learned.

Conditioned.

And once you understand where they come from—

you'll finally understand how to change them.

CHAPTER TWO

Attachment Styles: The Root of Your Patterns

Your patterns didn't start in your last relationship.

They didn't start with the person who hurt you the most.

They didn't even start when you began dating.

They started much earlier.

Before you knew what love was supposed to feel like.
Before you understood relationships.
Before you had the words to explain your emotions.

Your patterns began the moment you learned:

what love feels like...
what love requires...
and what love costs.

❧ What Is an Attachment Style?

Your attachment style is the way you:

- connect
- respond
- and behave in relationships

It's your emotional blueprint.

It determines:

- how safe you feel with others
- how you react to closeness
- how you handle distance
- how you respond to conflict

And most importantly—

it shapes what you **accept**, what you **fear**, and what you **chase**.

✦ Love Was Your First Teacher

Before you understood relationships—

you experienced them.

You learned:

- how attention was given
- how affection was shown
- how consistency (or inconsistency) felt

You learned whether love was:

✓ safe

✓ unpredictable

✓ conditional

✓ distant

And without realizing it—

you carried those lessons into your adult relationships.

 The Four Attachment Styles

There are four main attachment styles.

You may see yourself in one…
or a combination of more than one.

Secure Attachment

This is the foundation of healthy connection.

You feel:

✓ comfortable with closeness
✓ safe expressing your emotions
✓ trusting without losing yourself

You don't chase.
You don't avoid.

You choose.

Anxious Attachment

This style is rooted in fear of abandonment.

You may:

- overthink
- seek reassurance
- feel deeply affected by distance

Love can feel intense.

You want closeness—but you also fear losing it.

So you hold on tighter.

🐾 Avoidant Attachment

This style is rooted in fear of vulnerability.

You may:

- value independence over connection
- pull away when things get too close
- struggle to express emotions

Love can feel overwhelming.

So instead of leaning in—

you create space.

❋ Fearful-Avoidant Attachment

This is a mix of both.

You crave connection—

but fear it at the same time.

You may:

- move close… then pull away
- feel deeply, but struggle to trust
- want love, but resist it when it becomes real

This creates the push and pull dynamic.

The one that feels intense… but unstable.

✨ Why You Keep Repeating the Same Pattern

Your attachment style doesn't just influence how you love—

it influences who you choose.

You are drawn to people who:

- activate your emotions
- match your internal pattern
- feel familiar to your nervous system

Not necessarily people who are healthy for you.

People who feel **recognizable**.

✨ How Attachment Shows Up in Relationships

This is where it becomes real.

An anxious person may:

- chase reassurance
- overanalyze communication
- stay longer than they should

An avoidant person may:

- withdraw during conflict
- avoid emotional depth
- leave when things become serious

A fearful-avoidant person may:

- create intense connections
- then become distant
- then return again

And a secure person?

They don't play games.

They communicate.
They choose consistency.
They walk away from instability.

 **The Problem Isn't Just Them**

It's easy to point at the other person.

To say:

"They're distant."
"They're inconsistent."
"They're the problem."

But the deeper question is:

Why does this dynamic feel familiar to you?

Why does it feel hard to walk away?

Why does it feel like something you need to "fix"?

✨ Awareness Changes Everything

Once you understand your attachment style—

you begin to see your relationships differently.

You stop asking:

👉 "Why are they like this?"

And start asking:

👉 "Why am I drawn to this?"

🧩 You Are Not Stuck

Your attachment style is not your identity.

It's a pattern.

And patterns can change.

With awareness.
With intention.
With choice.

🧩 The Shift Begins Here

You don't need to become a different person.

You need to become a more **aware** version of yourself.

Because when you understand your attachment—

you stop reacting automatically.

You pause.

You reflect.

You choose differently.

🐾 A Moment of Reflection

Ask yourself:

- How do I respond when someone gets close to me?
- Do I lean in… or pull away?
- Do I feel safe in love—or uncertain?
- What do I fear most in relationships?

Your answers reveal your pattern.

🐾 What Comes Next

Now that you understand the root—

we're going to challenge something you've been taught to rely on.

Because while attachment explains your patterns—

there's another layer influencing your behavior.

One you've probably used to make sense of your relationships.

CHAPTER THREE

The Zodiac Illusion: What You Think Is the Problem

You've probably asked the question before.

"What sign are they?"

Before you ask how they communicate…
Before you ask how they love…
Before you ask what they're capable of emotionally—

you ask their sign.

Because somewhere along the way, you were taught:

☞ your sign explains your relationships
☞ your sign explains compatibility
☞ your sign explains why things work—or don't

And for a moment…

it feels like it makes sense.

🦋 When It Feels Like the Answer

You read something about your sign and think:

"That's exactly me."

You read about someone else's sign and think:

"That's exactly them."

And suddenly—

everything feels explained.

Why they pulled away.
Why they didn't communicate.
Why the connection didn't last.

It becomes easy to say:

☞ "That's just how they are."
☞ "We weren't compatible."
☞ "Our signs didn't match."

✦ But Something Still Doesn't Add Up

Because even with all that information—

the pattern doesn't change.

You still find yourself in similar situations.

Still feeling:

- confused
- emotionally drained
- unsure where things went wrong

Different signs.

Same outcome.

✦ The Illusion of Explanation

Zodiac can describe tendencies.

It can highlight:

- personality traits
- emotional expression
- communication styles

But it doesn't explain:

☞ why you stay in unhealthy situations
☞ why you ignore red flags
☞ why certain connections feel impossible to walk away from

✨ You've Been Looking in the Wrong Direction

It's easier to look at someone's sign…

than to look at your pattern.

Because your pattern requires:

- honesty
- awareness
- responsibility

And that's uncomfortable.

✨ Zodiac Doesn't Control Your Choices

You don't stay because of your sign.

You stay because something in you:

☞ feels attached
☞ feels familiar
☞ feels activated

✨ Compatibility Isn't the Problem

You can be "compatible" on paper…

and still experience:

- inconsistency
- emotional distance
- confusion

You can have:

✔ shared interests

✔ strong attraction

✔ deep conversations

And still feel:

✘ uncertain

✘ unfulfilled

✘ disconnected

🧩 Why the Pattern Keeps Repeating

Because you're not choosing based on alignment.

You're choosing based on:

👉 emotional activation

👉 familiarity

👉 attachment patterns

🧩 The Comfort of Believing It's the Sign

Blaming zodiac can feel comforting.

It gives you an explanation that doesn't require change.

It allows you to say:

☞ "It just wasn't meant to be."

Instead of asking:

☞ **"Why did I stay longer than I should have?"**

✨ This Is Where the Shift Happens

You don't have to reject zodiac.

You just have to understand its place.

It can:

✓ give insight
✓ offer perspective
✓ help you understand tendencies

But it cannot:

- ✖ explain your patterns
- ✖ determine your relationships
- ✖ replace self-awareness

✿ The Truth You Need to Hear

Your sign may influence how you express love.

But your attachment style determines:

- ☞ what you tolerate
- ☞ what you chase
- ☞ what you struggle to walk away from

✿ This Changes Everything

Because once you understand this—

you stop looking for answers outside of yourself.

You stop trying to figure out:

👉 who is compatible

And start understanding:

👉 **what pattern you're repeating**

✨ A Moment of Reflection

Ask yourself:

- Have I ever blamed a relationship outcome on zodiac?
- What patterns have repeated regardless of the person's sign?
- What have I avoided seeing about myself?

✨ What Comes Next

Now that you've separated the illusion from the truth—

it's time to bring both together.

Because while zodiac doesn't control your patterns—

it does influence how those patterns show up.

CHAPTER FOUR

When Attachment Meets Your Sign

By now, you understand two things:

Your attachment style shapes your patterns. Your zodiac sign reflects how you express yourself.

But this is where it becomes real—

What happens when the two come together?

 **It's Not One or the Other**

You are not just your sign.

And you are not just your attachment style.

You are both.

Your attachment style determines:

☞ what you fear

☞ what you seek

☞ what you tolerate

Your sign influences:

☞ how you express it

☞ how you react

☞ how you show up emotionally

And when these two combine—

they create your relationship behavior.

✧ Why Love Feels So Complicated

You may think:

☞ "This is just how I am."

☞ "That's just my sign."

But what you're experiencing is deeper than that.

It's your emotional pattern—

expressed through your personality.

🪶 The Same Pattern—Different Expression

Two people can have the same attachment style—

but behave completely differently.

Why?

Because their emotional expression is different.

🪶 Anxious Attachment

At the core:

You want closeness.
You want reassurance.
You want to feel secure.

44

But how that shows up depends on you.

If your nature is more emotional and intuitive—

you may:

- feel deeply
- overthink
- become overwhelmed

If your nature is more expressive and outward—

you may:

- seek attention
- need validation
- react more visibly

Same pattern.

Different expression.

✨ Avoidant Attachment Looks Different Too

At the core:

You value independence.
You protect your space.
You avoid emotional vulnerability.

But the way you do it can vary.

You may:

- become distant quietly
- avoid conversations
- or shift into logic instead of emotion

Or—

you may:

- come across as confident and detached
- keep things light
- avoid depth without realizing it

Same pattern.

Different behavior.

✨ Why This Matters in Relationships

Because you're not just experiencing someone's sign.

You're experiencing:

👉 their attachment style
👉 expressed through their personality

And if you don't understand that—

you misinterpret what's happening.

You think:

👉 "They just need time."
👉 "That's just how they are."

But what you're actually experiencing is:

👉 a pattern playing out in real time

🐾 When Patterns Collide

This is where relationships become intense.

When one person seeks closeness…

and the other pulls away.

When one person expresses emotions…

and the other avoids them.

When one person holds on…

and the other creates distance.

It creates a cycle:

- pursuit
- withdrawal
- confusion
- reconnection

Over and over again.

🐾 It Feels Like Chemistry—But It's a Pattern

That intense connection?

That emotional pull?

That feeling of *"I can't let this go"*?

It's not always alignment.

Sometimes—

it's your patterns interacting.

✨ You Start Misreading the Situation

Because you're looking at:

👉 personality
👉 attraction
👉 compatibility

Instead of:

👉 behavior
👉 consistency
👉 emotional capacity

And that's where confusion begins.

✨ The Real Question You Need to Ask

Not:

👉 "What sign are they?"

But:

👉 **"How do they show up emotionally?"**

Do they:

- stay consistent?
- communicate clearly?
- show up when it matters?

Or do they:

- pull away
- create uncertainty
- leave you questioning everything?

That answer tells you more than their sign ever will.

✤ This Is Where Your Awareness Deepens

Because now you understand:

It's not just who they are.

It's how they love.

And how they love—

must align with how you need to be loved.

✤ You Stop Being Confused by Behavior

Once you see this clearly—

you stop trying to make things fit.

You stop explaining inconsistency.

You stop chasing clarity.

Because you recognize the pattern.

 **A Moment of Reflection**

Ask yourself:

- What behaviors have I been excusing because of personality?
- What patterns have I mistaken for compatibility?
- How do I show up when I feel triggered?

Because the more honest you are here—

the more powerful your awareness becomes.

✤ What Comes Next

Now that you see how patterns and personality interact—

it's time to challenge something even deeper.

Because what you've been calling connection…

may not be what you think it is.

CHAPTER FIVE

Chemistry vs. Compatibility

It felt strong from the beginning.

The conversation flowed.
The connection felt easy.
There was a pull you couldn't explain.

And in that moment—

you believed something important:

"This must be real."

Because that's what we're taught.

If it feels strong…
If it feels intense…
If you can't stop thinking about them…

It must mean something.

But Feeling Something Doesn't Mean It's Right

Chemistry is powerful.

It can feel:

- exciting
- magnetic
- immediate

It can make you feel:

- seen

- understood
- connected

But chemistry is not always a sign of alignment.

Sometimes—

it's a sign of activation.

What Chemistry Really Is

Chemistry often comes from:

☞ familiarity
☞ emotional triggers
☞ unresolved patterns

It's your system recognizing something it already knows.

Not always something that's healthy—

but something that's familiar.

And familiar feels comfortable…

even when it leads to discomfort later.

Why It Feels So Real

Because it's intense.

And intensity creates the illusion of depth.

You feel everything quickly:

- connection
- attraction

*   emotion

But real connection doesn't rely on intensity.

It builds through consistency.

Compatibility Feels Different

Compatibility is quieter.

It doesn't overwhelm you.

It doesn't confuse you.

It feels:

*   steady

- clear
- consistent

It doesn't require you to question where you stand.

It shows you.

Why People Choose Chemistry Over Compatibility

Because chemistry is immediate.

You feel it right away.

Compatibility takes time.

You don't always recognize it at first—

because it doesn't create the same emotional rush.

But what feels calm…

is often what lasts.

When Chemistry Becomes a Cycle

If you rely only on chemistry—

you may find yourself repeating the same experience.

Strong beginning.

Intense connection.

Emotional shift.

Confusion.

Over and over again.

Because chemistry alone doesn't sustain a relationship.

You Can Have Chemistry Without Stability

This is the part most people don't realize.

You can feel deeply connected to someone—

and still not be able to build something real with them.

You can:

✓ laugh together
✓ talk for hours
✓ feel understood in moments

And still experience:

✗ inconsistency
✗ emotional distance
✗ lack of commitment

Compatibility Is About Alignment

It's not about how strong it feels.

It's about how well it works.

Do you both:

- communicate clearly?
- show up consistently?
- handle conflict in a healthy way?

Do your needs align?

Do your values match?

That's compatibility.

You Don't Have to Choose Intensity

You've been taught to chase what feels strong.

But what feels strong—

is not always what's right.

You can choose:

- ☞ stability over intensity
- ☞ clarity over confusion
- ☞ consistency over unpredictability

And that choice changes everything.

This Is Where Your Awareness Deepens

You begin to recognize:

Not everything that feels good—

is good for you.

And not everything that feels calm—

is boring.

Sometimes, calm is safe.

Sometimes, calm is aligned.

A Moment of Reflection

Ask yourself:

- What have I been calling chemistry?
- How has that feeling ended for me in the past?
- Have I overlooked compatibility because it didn't feel intense?

Because the answers will show you the difference.

Final Truth

Chemistry can pull you in.

But compatibility determines whether it lasts.

And once you understand that—

you stop chasing what feels intense…

and start choosing what feels right.

It felt strong.
But now you're learning what actually works.

CHAPTER SIX

Emotional Triggers and Relationship Cycles

It's not always what's happening.

It's what it brings up in you.

A message left unanswered.
A change in tone.
A shift in energy.

To someone else, it might not mean much.

But to you—

it feels like everything.

What Is an Emotional Trigger?

An emotional trigger is a reaction that feels stronger than the moment itself.

It's when something small…

creates a big emotional response.

Not because the moment is overwhelming—

but because it connects to something deeper.

Something you've felt before.

It's Not Just About Now

When you're triggered, you're not just reacting to the present.

You're reacting to:

- past experiences
- past emotions
- past patterns

That's why it feels so intense.

Because it's not just one moment.

It's many moments—stacked together.

How Triggers Show Up in Relationships

You may notice:

- overthinking small changes
- needing reassurance

- feeling anxious when things shift
- shutting down when emotions rise

And in those moments—

your response feels automatic.

Like you don't have time to think.

You just feel…

and react.

Your Attachment Style Drives the Reaction

If you lean anxious—

you may:

- seek reassurance
- overanalyze communication
- feel unsettled by distance

If you lean avoidant—

you may:

- pull away
- avoid emotional conversations
- create space when things feel intense

If you lean fearful—

you may:

- move closer… then pull back
- want connection… but resist it
- feel torn between staying and leaving

Different responses.

Same root.

The Cycle Begins Here

Trigger → Reaction → Response →
Outcome

You feel something.
You react to it.
They respond to your reaction.
And the cycle continues.

Until it becomes a pattern.

One that repeats itself—

even with different people.

You're Not Overreacting—You're Responding to Something Real

The feeling is real.

But the intensity…

may not match the moment.

And that's where awareness matters.

Because when you understand your triggers—

you don't ignore them.

You learn from them.

Triggers Reveal What Needs Attention

They show you:

- where you feel insecure
- where you feel uncertain
- where you need clarity

They're not the problem.

They're information.

The Difference Between Reaction and Response

A reaction is immediate.

It's emotional.
Automatic.
Unfiltered.

A response is intentional.

It's thoughtful.
Grounded.
Aware.

And the space between the two—

is where your power is.

You Don't Have to React the Same Way

Just because you feel something—

doesn't mean you have to act on it
immediately.

You can:

- pause
- breathe
- reflect

And choose how you want to respond.

This Is How the Cycle Changes

Not by avoiding triggers—

but by understanding them.

Because once you understand them—

you stop letting them control your behavior.

And that changes the outcome.

You Become More Aware of Yourself

You begin to notice:

- what sets you off
- how you usually respond
- what the pattern looks like

And that awareness creates space.

Space to do something different.

A Moment of Reflection

Ask yourself:

- What situations trigger me most in relationships?
- How do I usually respond when I feel triggered?
- What does that response create?

Because your answers reveal your cycle.

Final Truth

Your triggers don't define you.

But how you respond to them—

shapes your relationships.

And once you become aware of that—

you stop repeating the same emotional
cycle…

and start creating a different experience.

**It's not just what's happening.
It's how you're responding to it.**

CHAPTER SEVEN

The Push and Pull Dynamic

It doesn't feel steady.

One moment, everything feels right.

They're present.
Engaged.
Connected.

And just when you begin to relax—

something shifts.

They pull back.

Not completely.

Just enough to make you feel it.

And suddenly—

you're trying to understand what changed.

It Starts With Closeness

In the beginning, the connection feels
natural.

You talk.
You laugh.
You feel seen.

There's no confusion.

And that's what makes the shift so
noticeable.

Because you've experienced what it feels
like when things are good.

Then the Distance Begins

The communication changes.

The energy feels different.

They may:

- respond less

- become less available

- avoid deeper conversations

And instead of clarity—

you're left with questions.

You Move Closer When They Pull Away

When you feel the distance—

you try to close the gap.

You:

- reach out more

- try to reconnect

- look for reassurance

Not because you're trying too hard—

but because you felt the connection.

And you don't understand why it's
changing.

They Pull Away When It Gets Too Close

At the same time—

as things become more real…

they create space.

Not always intentionally.

But because closeness feels uncomfortable
for them.

So they:

- withdraw

- become less responsive

- avoid emotional depth

And the cycle continues.

This Is the Push and Pull

One person moves closer.

The other moves away.

And when one pulls back—

the other feels it.

So they move closer again.

And the pattern repeats.

It Feels Like a Connection You Can't Let Go Of

Because there are moments when it feels right.

Moments when they show up.

Moments when the connection returns.

And those moments keep you attached.

Because you know what it can feel like.

But It's Not Consistent

The connection comes and goes.

And over time—

that inconsistency becomes the experience.

Not the exception.

Why This Dynamic Feels So Strong

Because it activates both people.

One person's distance—

triggers the other's need for closeness.

And that closeness—

triggers the other's need for space.

It's not intentional.

But it's powerful.

This Is Where Attachment Styles Show Up Clearly

This dynamic often comes from:

☞ anxious attachment
☞ avoidant attachment

One seeks connection.

One protects distance.

And together—

they create a cycle that feels intense…

but unstable.

You Start Trying to Fix It

You think:

☞ "If I just understand them…"
☞ "If I give them space…"
☞ "If I show them I care…"

Then maybe things will stabilize.

But the pattern doesn't change—

because the root hasn't changed.

You're Not Meant to Stay in Cycles

You're not meant to:

- chase clarity

- feel uncertain

- question where you stand

Love is not supposed to feel like a constant adjustment.

This Is Where Awareness Breaks the Cycle

Once you recognize the push and pull—

you stop reacting the same way.

You stop:

- chasing when they pull away

- overextending to fix things

- ignoring how it feels

You begin to:

- observe

- pause

- choose differently

The Cycle Only Continues If You Participate

This is the truth most people don't want to face.

The pattern continues—

because both people are engaged in it.

But once one person changes their response—

the cycle shifts.

Or it ends.

A Moment of Reflection

Ask yourself:

- When someone pulls away, how do I respond?

- Do I move closer—or step back?

- What has this dynamic created in my past relationships?

Because your response determines whether the pattern continues.

Final Truth

The push and pull feels like connection.

But it's a cycle.

And once you see it clearly—

you stop chasing what moves away from you…

and start choosing what stays.

It felt real.
But now you understand what it actually is.

CHAPTER EIGHT

Awareness: Seeing the Pattern Clearly

There's a moment when everything becomes clear.

Not because something new happens—

but because you finally see what's been there all along.

The pattern.

The behavior.

The way it made you feel.

And once you see it clearly—

you can't unsee it.

It Doesn't Feel the Same Anymore

What once felt exciting…

now feels draining.

What once felt like connection…

now feels inconsistent.

What once felt like possibility…

now feels familiar.

And that shift?

It's not confusion.

It's awareness.

You Stop Explaining Things Away

Before—

you found reasons to stay.

You told yourself:

- "Maybe thcy're just busy."
- "Maybe I'm overthinking."
- "Maybe I just need to give it time."

But now—

you don't feel the need to explain
everything.

Because you understand something deeper:

You shouldn't have to explain what doesn't feel right.

The Pattern Becomes Obvious

You start to see:

- how it started
- how it shifted
- how it repeated

And instead of seeing separate moments—

you see a cycle.

A cycle that no longer feels accidental.

A cycle that now feels clear.

You Feel the Shift Within Yourself

This awareness isn't just mental.

It's emotional.

You feel:

- more grounded
- less reactive
- more aware of what you're experiencing

Not because everything is resolved—

but because you're no longer ignoring it.

You Stop Holding Onto the Beginning

You no longer cling to:

- how it felt at first
- what it could have been
- the version of the connection you hoped for

Because you're focused on what it is.

And what it is—

is no longer aligned.

Clarity Removes the Illusion

You're not guessing anymore.

You're not overanalyzing.

You're not trying to make it make sense.

Because it already does.

And that clarity…

removes the illusion.

This Is Where Your Power Returns

Confusion keeps you stuck.

But clarity—

gives you direction.

It allows you to:

- step back
- reflect
- choose differently

Without needing more answers.

You Realize It's Not Yours to Fix

For a long time—

you may have tried to fix the situation.

To understand it.

To make it work.

But now—

you see something different.

It's not yours to fix.

You Don't Need More Time

You don't need:

- more conversations
- more explanations
- more waiting

Because awareness doesn't come from time.

It comes from truth.

And you already have it.

This Is the Turning Point

This is where everything changes.

Not because the situation changes—

but because you do.

You stop:

- chasing clarity
- ignoring your feelings
- holding onto what isn't stable

And you start:

- trusting yourself
- seeing things as they are
- choosing what aligns with you

A Moment of Reflection

Ask yourself:

- What have I been trying to make sense of that already feels clear?
- Where have I been holding on to what no longer feels right?
- What am I now ready to see differently?

Because your answers…

will guide your next step.

Final Truth

Nothing new happened.

You just finally saw it clearly.

And once you see clearly—

you don't move the same.

You don't stay the same.

And you don't repeat the same.

**This is the moment everything shifts.
And from here—you begin to choose
differently.**

CHAPTER NINE

Choosing Differently

Seeing the pattern is one thing.

Choosing differently…

is something else.

Because even when you understand what's
happening—

you may still feel the pull.

The urge to go back.
To check in.
To respond the way you always have.

And that's where the real work begins.

Awareness Doesn't Remove the Feeling

You may still:

- think about them
- miss what it felt like
- feel connected to the experience

That doesn't mean you should return to it.

It means you're human.

Because patterns don't disappear overnight.

They change through choice.

The Moment You Pause

Before—

you reacted.

You responded quickly.

You followed the feeling.

Now—

you pause.

And that pause changes everything.

Because in that moment—

you create space.

Space between:

👉 what you feel
👉 and what you choose to do

You Don't Have to Follow the Pattern

Just because something feels familiar—

doesn't mean you have to repeat it.

You can feel the pull—

and still choose something different.

You can miss the connection—

and still walk away.

You can want clarity—

and still stop chasing it.

You Start Asking Different Questions

Instead of asking:

👉 "Why are they like this?"

You ask:

👉 "What am I choosing right now?"

That shift—

brings your power back to you.

You Stop Moving From Emotion Alone

Before—

your choices were driven by feeling.

Now—

they're guided by awareness.

You consider:

- what feels right
- what aligns with you
- what supports your growth

Not just what feels good in the moment.

You Don't Need Immediate Answers

You don't need:

- a response
- a conversation

- an explanation

To make a different choice.

Because clarity is already there.

You're just choosing to follow it.

You Start Choosing Yourself

In small ways.

You:

- stop overexplaining
- stop overextending
- stop engaging in what feels unclear

Not to prove anything—

but to protect your peace.

This Is Where Your Standard Changes

You begin to recognize:

☞ what you're no longer willing to accept

And once you know that—

you don't go back to it.

Even when it feels familiar.

Choosing Differently Feels Uncomfortable—At First

Because it's new.

You're no longer:

- chasing
- reacting
- trying to fix things

You're simply choosing…

not to engage the same way.

And that can feel unfamiliar.

But unfamiliar doesn't mean wrong.

It means you're growing.

You Don't Have to Explain Your Choice

You don't need to:

- justify it
- explain it
- defend it

Your clarity is enough.

Your awareness is enough.

The Pattern Changes When You Do

The cycle doesn't continue—

when you stop participating in it.

When you:

- don't respond the same way
- don't chase the same way
- don't stay the same way

Everything shifts.

Or it ends.

A Moment of Reflection

Ask yourself:

- What have I been choosing out of habit?
- What would it look like to choose differently?
- What am I ready to stop repeating?

Because your answers—

are your next step.

Final Truth

Change doesn't happen all at once.

It happens in moments.

Moments where you pause.
Moments where you reflect.
Moments where you choose differently.

And those moments—

create a new pattern.

You don't break the cycle by
understanding it alone.
You break it by choosing differently.

CHAPTER TEN

Becoming the Version of You That Loves Better

You don't go back to who you were.

Not after this.

Not after you've seen it clearly.

Because once you understand your patterns—

once you recognize your triggers—

once you see how you've been choosing—

you don't move the same anymore.

This Isn't About Perfection

You're not going to get everything right.

You may still feel:

- moments of doubt

- moments of pull

- moments of uncertainty

But something is different now.

You're aware.

And awareness changes everything.

You Start Moving With Intention

Before—

your choices were automatic.

Now—

they're intentional.

You pause.

You reflect.

You choose.

Not based on habit—

but based on alignment.

You Stop Abandoning Yourself

You don't ignore what you feel anymore.

You don't silence your needs.

You don't stay in situations that make you
question your worth.

Because you understand something now:

**how you show up for yourself
shapes every relationship you experience.**

You Redefine What Love Feels Like

Love is no longer:

- confusing

- inconsistent

- emotionally draining

Love becomes:

✓ clear
✓ steady
✓ supportive

It doesn't leave you questioning where you stand.

It shows you.

You Recognize What Doesn't Align

You see it faster.

The inconsistency.
The emotional distance.
The patterns that once pulled you in.

And instead of trying to make it work—

you step back.

Because you no longer need to prove
anything.

You Don't Chase What's Meant for You

You don't:

- overextend

- overexplain

- overinvest

You allow things to unfold.

And if something requires you to lose yourself—

you let it go.

This Is What Growth Looks Like

Not forcing.
Not chasing.
Not trying to fix everything.

But choosing:

- clarity

- alignment

- self-respect

Again and again.

You Become the Standard

You no longer look outside of yourself for answers.

You don't rely on:

- signs

- labels

- assumptions

You trust what you feel.

You trust what you see.

You trust yourself.

You Create Space for Something Real

When you stop holding onto what isn't right—

you create space.

For something that:

- meets you

- respects you

- aligns with you

Not through intensity—

but through consistency.

This Is Where Everything Changes

Not overnight.

But over time.

Through your choices.

Through your awareness.

Through your willingness to do something different.

A Moment of Reflection

Ask yourself:

- Who am I becoming in the way I love?

- What am I no longer willing to accept?

- What does a healthy relationship feel like to me now?

Because your answers…

shape your future.

Final Truth

You don't need to become someone new.

You just need to become more aware of who you are.

Because the more you understand yourself—

the better you choose.

And the better you choose—

the different your life becomes.

You didn't need a different sign.
You needed a different level of awareness.

www.ingramcontent.com/pod-product-compliance
Lightning Source LLC
Chambersburg PA
CBHW071311030726
47594CB00002B/384